An organizer to make your Christmas season meaningful complete with convenient printable resources!

Treasuring the Season

Leanne Phelps and Mike Brown

Treasuring the Season:
A Christmas Organizer and Devotional
by
Leanne Phelps and Mike Brown

Published by
OneHope Publishing

Illustrations by
Jelena Radevic,
MilaWorldDesign
www.etsy.com/shop/MilaWorldDesign

Designed by
Katrina M Tardibono
@TardibonoGraphics
https://www.behance.net/tardibonographics

Printed and Distributed by
Kindle Direct Publishing
ISBN 978-0-9976300-4-6

It's the Christmas season! It's such an exciting time of the year. We are so grateful to God for the gift of His Son and we always want that to be the focus of the season. The anticipation of Christmas Day is part of the joy of this special season, too!

This book is intended to help with the focus and also with the anticipation. It has 25 devotions to be read each day of December leading up to and including Christmas. Each day also has some ideas for gifts, traditions, decorations and more. There are also sections for checklists, recipes, address organizer, calendars, printables, and more. You can use this as a one-time season planner or make notes and use it year after year. You can make copies of the pages of this book for your personal use, as well. We hope this book helps keep you organized and that it builds excitement for the season celebrating the best gift ever given--the gift of Jesus!

THIS BOOK BELONGS TO

_____

Day 1

At Christmas, we frequently hear the term "Messiah." It is a Hebrew word meaning "anointed one." Its equivalent in Greek (the language of the original New Testament) is *Christos*, or *Christ* in English. From earliest times, a person was envisioned who would save or redeem God's people to Him. After the fall of mankind in Genesis 3, God pronounced a curse on creation. In the midst of the curse, God promised One who would redeem mankind from the curse and the power of the serpent:

Genesis 3:15 (NKJV)
15 And I will put enmity between you [the serpent] and the woman, And between your seed and her Seed; He shall bruise your head, And you shall bruise His heel."

This *seed* speaks of "he" we would later call Messiah. "Seed" implies a lineage leading to Messiah. Many centuries and generations into this lineage, we encounter Abraham. God confirmed the perpetuation of this lineage with Abraham. In the New Testament, Paul wrote this about that:

Galatians 3:16 (NKJV)
16 Now to Abraham and his Seed were the promises made. He does not say, "And to seeds," as of many, but as of one, "And to your Seed," who is Christ.

Messiah was universally anticipated among the Jewish people. The Old Testament prophets predicted him. The psalms spoke of him repeatedly. Hebrew worship practices instituted by God through Moses pointed to Him symbolically. By the time of Jesus, prophetic timelines seemed to converge and the air was buzzing with messianic expectation.

"Messiah" hoisted the banner of several roles given in scripture. The role most prominent and most popular was that of a conquering, king. The Jews of Jesus' day were looking for a temporal leader who would stamp out Roman tyranny and establish his own kingdom in Israel. They did not recognize their spiritual need. They did not conceive of a savior coming twice, as we do today, so they could not distinguish between his first purpose and his second purpose. That first purpose was to become the means of spiritual, eternal salvation. Jesus' first purpose was not recognized, so they did not accept him as their anointed one, their Messiah. This is the very important political context of that first Christmas. Today we see the big picture, and rejoice in God's grand purpose. Let's anticipate anew the celebration of the birth of Messiah, the Christ, with hopeful eyes on his second ultimate purpose of eternal, loving sovereignty and oversight, yet to be fulfilled.

Personal Reflections

_____

_____

_____

_____

_____

_____

_____

Holiday Checklist

4+ weeks before

- Create a Budget for the season
- Make shopping lists for gifts you need to buy
- Buy Christmas cards, stamps, wrapping supplies
- Make any travel plans
- Set up decorations or at least get them ready to put out
- Start advent calendar

3 weeks before

- Decorate Christmas tree
- Finish shopping for gifts
- Mail Christmas cards
- Finalize Christmas plans for parties, Christmas Eve, Christmas Day
- Finalize menus for your holiday meals

2 weeks before

- Wrap all gifts
- Plan Christmas attire
- Mail gifts going to out of town family and friends
- Could purchase non-perishable grocery items if desired

1 week before

- Shop for groceries
- Clean and prepare the house
- Make sure you have your phone or cameras charged and ready
- Read the Christmas Story together

Day 2

Hope of the Season

The Bible is full of genealogies. Usually, most of us tend to skip over them. Yet, they are very important to the identity of the Messiah. Both the Gospel of Mathew and the Gospel of Luke present a genealogy of Jesus. Matthew's genealogy (chapter 1) begins with Abraham, continuing through David down to Joseph, the husband of Mary. Luke's genealogy (chapter 3) is presented in reverse, from Jesus backwards through David and Abraham, but continuing back all the way to Adam. The two lineages between Abraham and David are Identical. However, between David and Jesus they are different. Luke's listing is understood by most Bible students to be the lineage of Mary. Both Joseph (Jesus legal lineage) and Mary (his covenant lineage) were the offspring of David by two different branches of the family tree.

Several Old Testament prophecies would confirm the messianic lineage up to a certain point in time. The inclusion of David was such a case. Many false Messiahs would come, both before and after Jesus. Thus, appropriate genealogies were an important validating credential for the Messiah. Jesus was often referred to as the *Son of David*. Now, as you read these genealogies, or maybe read past them, at least see them as important messianic qualifiers. The Bible is based on historical facts, often with supporting evidence. The first Christmas was historical reality. This is what we celebrate.

Personal Reflections

Advent Calendars

Advent Calendars can be as simple as the cardboard ones with a piece of chocolate behind the doors or as elaborate as one can imagine! Either way, the idea is the same—celebrating the anticipation of Christmas.

FUN ADVENT CALENDAR OPTIONS:

- Store bought candy calendars

- Paper chains made out of construction paper

- Handmade Calendars with 24 Christmas activities (make cookies together, go look at lights, etc.). You can use a ribbon with clothes pins to pin your daily idea on a long ribbon and hang it up.

- Handmade Calendars with 24 Bible verses counting down until Christmas

- A pile of 24 Christmas themed books to read one per night

- Store bought calendars with toys/legos/etc. inside each door

- Make an advent jar with a decorated mason jar and fill it with 24 mini cards, each with a scripture, a blessing you can do for someone else, an activity, etc.

- "Reverse" Advent Calendar— take an empty basket and add something to it each day to donate to a food bank or local shelter

- Cut out a large felt tree and 24 small felt circles to put on it, one per day

Day 3

Hope of the Season

In the times of the Old Testament, one of the unique and wonderful blessings given to Israel, as God's special called-out nation, was prophecy. God revealed Himself and His plans to Israel through the prophets. Prophets predicted God's agenda of redemption. The major theme of the prophets was the future coming of Messiah. Approximately 750 years before Jesus was born, Isaiah was given this prophecy.

Isaiah 9:6-7 (ESV) *6 For to us a child is born, to us a son is given; and the government shall be upon his shoulder, and his name shall be called Wonderful Counselor, Mighty God, Everlasting Father, Prince of Peace. 7 Of the increase of his government and of peace there will be no end, on the throne of David and over his kingdom, to establish it and to uphold it with justice and with righteousness from this time forth and forevermore. The zeal of the LORD of hosts will do this.*

Often quoted at Christmas, this very familiar passage pointed forward to Messiah. He would be born as a child. Note his titles include *Mighty God, Everlasting Father*. This prophecy proclaimed him as divine. Divine, yet born human. The profound incarnation of God in flesh was clearly foretold. Note also that the complete fulfillment of this prophecy stretches into our future--*forevermore*. Since the forecast about the incarnation was correct, we can be certain the future predictions of an everlasting kingdom will be accurate also. This is the hope Jesus brings, the hope Peter foresaw when he wrote:

2 Peter 1:19 (ESV)
19 And we have the prophetic word more fully confirmed, to which you will do well to pay attention as to a lamp shining in a dark place, until the day dawns and the morning star rises in your hearts,

Personal Reflections

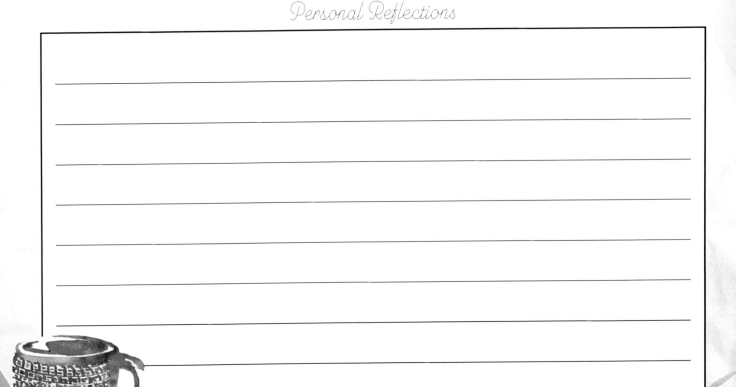

Jesse Tree

The Jesse Tree tradition is based on the verse in Isaiah 11:1 that says, "There shall come forth a shoot from the stump of Jesse..." It's a way to tell the story of God's plan for Jesus since the beginning of time. You can google this and find so many amazing ideas, books, ornament kits, etc. to start your own Jesse tree. Check etsy and Pinterest and you won't be disappointed. Or you can make your own ornament set using the symbols for the Jesse Tree:

1. A globe or picture of earth
2. An apple or snake
3. An ark
4. A camel
5. A lamb
6. A ladder
7. A coat of many colors
8. A tablet with ten numbers
9. A cluster of grapes
10. A sheaf of wheat
11. A slingshot
12. A Bible or scroll
13. A green leaf
14. A lion and a lamb
15. A dove and a crown
16. A lamb and staff
17. A cross
18. A heart
19. A Bethlehem town with a star
20. A fiery furnace
21. A brick wall
22. A star
23. A candle
24. An angel
25. A baby in a manger

Day 4

Hope of the Season

What is prophecy? Who are the Old Testament prophets that spoke of things to come? Several Old Testament Hebrew titles for prophets come from root words meaning, "speaks by inspiration", "shepherd" and "watchman" (one who peers into the distance). Several biblical passages help us better understand the source and inspiration of prophecy:

Numbers 12:6 (ESV)
⁶ And he said, "Hear my words: If there is a prophet among you, I the LORD make myself known to him in a vision; I speak with him in a dream.

2 Peter 1:20-21 (ESV)
²⁰ knowing this first of all, that no prophecy of Scripture comes from someone's own interpretation. ²¹ For no prophecy was ever produced by the will of man, but men spoke from God as they were carried along by the Holy Spirit.

1 Peter 1:10-12 (ESV)
¹⁰ Concerning this salvation, the prophets who prophesied about the grace that was to be yours searched and inquired carefully, ¹¹ inquiring what person or time the Spirit of Christ in them was indicating when he predicted the sufferings of Christ and the subsequent glories. ¹² It was revealed to them that they were serving not themselves but you, in the things that have now been announced to you through those who preached the good news to you by the Holy Spirit sent from heaven, things into which angels long to look.

The prophets and their messages were highly revered by kings and servants. Through the prophets, we have the very oracles of God about specific matters of life. The most vital theme of the prophetic messages was about One who would come from God, the One often called *Messiah*. In addition to the written and spoken prophesies, God also spoke of Messiah through benchmark historical events such as Passover and the swallowing of Jonah for three days and nights by the great sea monster. Additionally, God spoke in symbolic worship practices prescribed by Him, to Moses. Not all written prophecies are contained in the books of prophecy; some are in the psalms or other writings. After his resurrection, Jesus appeared to his disciples and said this:

Luke 24:44-45 (ESV)
⁴⁴ Then he said to them, "These are my words that I spoke to you while I was still with you, that everything written about me in the Law of Moses and the Prophets and the Psalms must be fulfilled." ⁴⁵ Then he opened their minds to understand the [Old Testament] Scripture . . .

Personal Reflections

_____
_____
_____
_____
_____
_____
_____
_____

Stocking Stuffer Ideas

Lip balm
Pens or pencils
Money
Gift cards
Favorite candy
Pez dispenser
Gum
Ornament
Postage stamps
Batteries
Nail polish
Make up
Silly string
Hair brush
Key chain
Small framed photo
Jewelry
Notepads
Thank you notes
Desk supplies
Travel sized shampoo
Travel sized lotion
Magnets
Small flashlight
Kitchen utensils
Flower seeds
Gloves
Hat
Pocket warmers
Socks
Slippers
Small stuffed animal
New wallet
Ear buds
Sunglasses

_____

_____

_____

_____

_____

_____

_____

_____

_____

_____

_____

_____

_____

Day 5

Isaiah 49:5-6 (ESV)
5 And now the LORD says, he who formed me from the womb to be his servant, to bring Jacob back to him; and that Israel might be gathered to him— for I am honored in the eyes of the LORD, and my God has become my strength—
6 he says: "It is too light a thing that you should be my servant to raise up the tribes of Jacob and to bring back the preserved of Israel; I will make you as a light for the nations, that my salvation may reach to the end of the earth."

Long before Jesus was born in Bethlehem, Isaiah the prophet was given this prophetic statement of the Son expressing his purpose as conveyed from the Father. What a profound and precious dialog we have recorded between the Father and the Son. It is the Father who brings the panoramic scope to the work of the Son, who would be formed in the womb. Jesus was born to be the Savior of the world, Jews and Gentiles from all nations. This is totally reason for Christmas Joy.

Personal Reflections

Family Traditions

It's fun to have a family tradition—something the whole family will remember for years to come! If you don't have a current tradition, it's not too late to start one! Here are a few suggestions for fun family traditions:

- Build an annual gingerbread house
- Watch a Christmas movie together
- Go to an annual Christmas Eve service
- Go together to look at Christmas lights
- Prepare Christmas gifts to pass out to neighbors
- Open new Christmas pajamas every Christmas eve
- Pick a night for the family to sleep under the tree
- Host an annual gathering for friends or family during the season
- Read the Christmas story from the Bible every Christmas morning
- Take turns putting the star or angel on the top of the tree
- Make Christmas cookies together
- Have a big Christmas shopping day or evening together as a family
- Decorate the tree together
- Christmas sing-along around the piano
- Do an advent calendar
- Host an ornament exchange or a cookie exchange

Our traditions

When the angel Gabriel announced to Mary that she was to give birth to the Son of God, she responded in this way.

Luke 1:38 (NKJV)
Then Mary said, "Behold the maidservant of the Lord! Let it be to me according to your word." And the angel departed from her.

Can you imagine the impact of this announcement on Mary? She had to realize the social implications of being unmarried and pregnant in that strict Jewish culture. How would Joseph, her betrothed husband, accept this? Yet, she also grasped the unique privilege and blessing. She submitted to the message willingly.

While she was frightened and bewildered by the sudden, startling encounter with Gabriel, her willingness to accept this unsettling role was not settled by an impulsive decision made in a swirl of confusion. She was already fully committed to God's purposes. She knew the Old Testament scriptures, as we witness shortly afterwards. She called herself *a maidservant of the Lord,* indicating a predisposition of faith, humility and obedience. She was already fully committed to God.

We each must arm ourselves for obedience as we face the unexpected turns of daily reality. We do so by the predisposition of our will to serve the Lord, as Mary did. Just as a law-enforcement officer or a combat soldier is trained to respond to surprise and fear with a certain protocol, so should we be spiritually trained by diligent and devoted preparation. Are you in training for loving and serving God in every way?

Personal Reflections

Gifts to Make and Give

It can be fun to make something handmade to share with others around you! Neighbors, friends, and family members always appreciate a thoughtful gift that comes from the heart! Here are a few of our family's favorite homemade gifts to give:

- Brown Sugar Hand Scrub
- Christmas Stovetop Potpourri
- Candied Pecans
- Chex Mix
- Peanut Brittle
- Homemade Cinnamon Rolls
- Handmade to/from labels
- Cookie Mix in a Jar

 Printables available in the back of this book.

My personal favorties

_____

_____

_____

_____

_____

_____

_____

_____

Day 7

Hope of the Season

Matthew 1:20-23 (ESV)
²⁰ But as he considered these things, behold, an angel of the Lord appeared to him in a dream, saying, "Joseph, son of David, do not fear to take Mary as your wife, for that which is conceived in her is from the Holy Spirit. ²¹ She will bear a son, and you shall call his name Jesus, for he will save his people from their sins." ²² All this took place to fulfill what the Lord had spoken by the prophet: ²³ "Behold, the virgin shall conceive and bear a son, and they shall call his name Immanuel" (which means, God with us).

God with us. In Old Testament times, God dwelled with the Israelites in their wondering in the wilderness as a pillar of cloud by day and a pillar of fire by night. He dwelt between the sculptured cherubim in the tabernacle's Most Holy Place. He was near, but not too near. His presence was always behind a veil or separated at a specified distance from the people. Worshippers were forbidden to enter the Holy Place or the Most Holy Place. The tabernacle (and later, the temple) structure with its curtains of partition sent a clear message. God was holy and they were not, resulting in a perpetual separation from His immediate presence. With the coming of Jesus, we now have God with us. He is no longer at a distance or hidden from view. He came so near that he became a microscopic fetus in Mary's womb. He became a close friend to his disciples. John and Paul later wrote:

1 John 1:1,3b (ESV)
¹ That which was from the beginning, which we have heard, which we have seen with our eyes, which we looked upon and have touched with our hands, concerning the word of life—. . . ³ᵇ we proclaim also to you, so that you too may have fellowship with us; and indeed our fellowship is with the Father and with his Son Jesus Christ.

Ephesians 2:19 (ESV)
¹⁹ So then you are no longer strangers and aliens, but you are fellow citizens with the saints and members of the household of God,

Christmas initiates a new era of privilege for people of faith. It signals a new intimacy with God. No longer is God aloof. Through faith, Jesus makes God approachable, One who can be known and fellowshipped with. Joy to the World!

Personal Reflections

_____

_____

_____

_____

_____

_____

_____

Serving Others

The holidays can be a great time to serve others!

Not everyone has a big family around to celebrate with so be on the lookout for someone in your circle (church, school, neighborhood) that might appreciate an invite to church, to a Christmas party, a holiday movie, or even a meal on Christmas Day. Is there someone that isn't able to get home this year? Maybe lost a parent or loved one or an important relationship this year?

This is a great time to take Christmas goodies or go Christmas caroling at a local nursing home or assisted living location. Just call the activities coordinator and see if you can come by for a visit or if they have something already going on where they could use your help.

Many places this time of year are collecting coats and winter clothing for those in need. Consider going through your coats before the coldest weather hits and donate to a shelter or charity that could use them. There are often some great deals for Black Friday so think about picking up a coat at a bargain and donating a new coat to someone who could really use it.

Toy drives are fun and a great way to spread some cheer this season. Check out churches, Angel Trees, local charities, etc. and find a place to donate toys for kids in need.

If you are making a casserole or hot meal, double your recipe and text a neighbor to tell them you are sending dinner over so take the night off!

Day 8

Hope of the Season

Intertwined with Jesus' nativity narrative in the Gospel of Luke is the telling of another miraculous birth. Zechariah was a devout priest in Judah. He and his wife Elizabeth were old and had no children. Elizabeth was a relative of Mary of Nazareth. Once, Zechariah was on duty, burning incense in the temple when the angel Gabriel stood before him and announced that Elizabeth would have a son in her old age. The child would be a man of God, a forerunner having the spirit of Elijah. He was to be named John. Elizabeth did conceive and when she was in her sixth month, that is when Gabriel made his announcement to Mary. During that annunciation, Gabriel told Mary about her cousin Elizabeth being also miraculously pregnant.

Luke 1:39-45 (ESV)
39 In those days Mary arose and went with haste into the hill country, to a town in Judah, 40 and she entered the house of Zechariah and greeted Elizabeth. 41 And when Elizabeth heard the greeting of Mary, the baby leaped in her womb. And Elizabeth was filled with the Holy Spirit, 42 and she exclaimed with a loud cry, "Blessed are you among women, and blessed is the fruit of your womb! 43 And why is this granted to me that the mother of my Lord should come to me? 44 For behold, when the sound of your greeting came to my ears, the baby in my womb leaped for joy. 45 And blessed is she who believed that there would be a fulfillment of what was spoken to her from the Lord."

John the Baptist and Jesus were spiritually connected from the womb. John's great ministry paved the way for Jesus' emergence. They never met face-to-face until the day Jesus came to John to be baptized by him in the Jordan river. Yet, when John first laid eyes upon Jesus . . .

John 1:26-29 (ESV)
29 The next day he [John the Baptist] saw Jesus coming toward him, and said, "Behold, the Lamb of God, who takes away the sin of the world!

Behold indeed! This is for sure someone to behold. Jesus was born in Bethlehem to become our sacrificial lamb, the true atoning sacrifice for sin. John knew that through his spirit of prophecy. The same message is being proclaimed to us in New Testament scripture and applied to our hearts by God's Holy Spirit working in us to understand and embrace. This begins at Christmas.

Personal Reflections

A Book a Day!

A fun family activity, especially for families with young kids is to accumulate 12 or 24 Christmas themed books. Wrap all books up in wrapping paper, one by one. During the Christmas season, each night before bed, let the kids choose a book to unwrap and then read it together. This is a great Christmas countdown, plus it builds excitement about reading and books and that's always a great idea!

Here are a few titles to get you started:

The Berenstain Bears and the Joy of Giving, Jan Berenstain

The Tale of Three Trees, Angela Elwell Hunt

The Night Before Christmas, Charles Santore

The Snowman, Raymond Briggs

How the Grinch Stole Christmas, Dr. Suess

The Jolly Christmas Postman, Allan and Janet Ahlberg

God Gave Us Christmas, Lisa Tawn Bergren & David Hohn

The Pine Tree Parable, Liz Curtis Higgs

The Snowy Day, Ezra Jack Keats

Day 9

Hope of the Season

After her annunciation from Gabriel and learning the corresponding news about Elizabeth's miraculous pregnancy, she visited her cousin. After Mary and Elizabeth exchanged spirit-filled greetings, Mary spoke these words of praise, often referred to as Mary's Song:

Luke 1:46-55 (ESV)
⁴⁶ And Mary said, "My soul magnifies the Lord, ⁴⁷ and my spirit rejoices in God my Savior, ⁴⁸ for he has looked on the humble estate of his servant. For behold, from now on all generations will call me blessed; ⁴⁹ for he who is mighty has done great things for me, and holy is his name. ⁵⁰ And his mercy is for those who fear him from generation to generation. ⁵¹ He has shown strength with his arm; he has scattered the proud in the thoughts of their hearts; ⁵² he has brought down the mighty from their thrones and exalted those of humble estate; ⁵³ he has filled the hungry with good things, and the rich he has sent away empty. ⁵⁴ He has helped his servant Israel, in remembrance of his mercy, ⁵⁵ as he spoke to our fathers, to Abraham and to his offspring forever."

How can Mary magnify the Lord who is already infinite? We cannot magnify His being and essence, but we can magnify our perception and appreciation of those characteristics, and that is what she is doing. At Christmas especially, it is easy to let the crush of activities and schedules dominate our agendas. Mary reminds us to keep God's glory as the main thing.

Notice her emphasis on humility and her denunciation of pride. She speaks of personal humility and collective humility from the people of God. Jesus came into humble surroundings, emphasizing for us his own humility. He first experienced this attitude from his mother. With humble hearts, may we put our personal priorities behind the biggest priority of magnifying him.

Personal Reflections

_____

_____

_____

_____

_____

_____

_____

Christmas Memories on the Tree

If you have meaningful ornaments, when you are decorating the tree, tell the stories behind them! As you put it on the tree, tell about the person who made the ornament for you. Or maybe what your child was like the year they brought that "masterpiece" home from preschool. Or share about your first apartment when you see the ornaments from your first tree. If you have ornaments passed down from parents or grandparents, share a little about them as you place their ornaments on the tree.

Day 10

Hope of the Season

'O little town of Bethlehem how still we see thee lie.' So begins the well-known and beloved Christmas Carrol. Bethlehem was (and is) a village located just about four miles from Jerusalem. Is there significance in the town Bethlehem, or did it just randomly happen to be the place?

1000 years before Jesus, Bethlehem was the birthplace of David, of whom both Mary and Joseph were both descendants. It was located in the land of the tribe of Judah. Long before that, when Jacob pronounced the prophetic destiny of each of his twelve sons, he said this about Judah"

Genesis 49:10 (ESV)
10 The scepter shall not depart from Judah, nor the ruler's staff from between his feet, until tribute comes to him; and to him shall be the obedience of the peoples.

When the magi came to Jerusalem looking for the new king, Herod inquired of the religious leaders.

Matthew 2:4-6 (ESV)
4 and assembling all the chief priests and scribes of the people, he inquired of them where the Christ was to be born. 5 They told him, "In Bethlehem of Judea, for so it is written by the prophet: 6 "'And you, O Bethlehem, in the land of Judah, are by no means least among the rulers of Judah; for from you shall come a ruler who will shepherd my people Israel.'"

Micah, the prophet they were quoting, prophesied about 300 years after David, 700 years before Jesus. Messiah would be a descendant of Judah and further, of David, born in Bethlehem according to Jewish prophecy. The profound mystery of prophesy pinpointed this detail.

Responding to Caesar's decree to be registered, Mary and Joseph journeyed from Nazareth to Bethlehem because they were of the lineage of David. Thus, they fulfilled those prophecies. Throughout his earthly presence, Jesus was often called "Son of David," even being born in Bethlehem, David's town.

Personal Reflections

_____

_____

_____

_____

_____

_____

_____

_____

_____

Gingerbread Houses

A gingerbread house can be fun for the whole family, especially if you purchase some candy favorites to decorate with (and to eat).

For littlest kids, instead of a house, just use an upside-down sugar ice cream cone and decorate it as a Christmas tree. Just use green icing, red pull apart Twizzlers for the garland, and sprinkles and M&Ms for the ornaments.

Another young kid option is to make the houses out of graham crackers. Use pre-made royal icing to put the house together or for a super easy (but non-edible) option, hot glue the graham crackers together and to a paper plate for ultimate in sturdiness! Just have extra graham crackers available for munching.

For all ages, there are so many great gingerbread house kits available. You can purchase one and then ask each family member to choose one candy option to purchase in addition to it. That way there is way more candy than needed (which is good) and everyone has something they love to snack on along the way.

If you feel super adventurous, you can make your own gingerbread and your own royal icing. It's not easy, but it's rewarding, and it tastes WAY better than kits or pre-made gingerbread. Be prepared to have to give it a few tries the first time you do it, but this is a sure-fire way to start a really impressive family tradition.

Tip: Instead of pouring whole bags of candy into bowls to decorate with, consider using ice cube trays to put small amounts of each candy in the sections and giving a tray to each person. This will help prevent ruining a whole bag of something yummy when a little icing-covered hand reaches in the bag! And also helps with the "sharing."

If you love making gingerbread houses, host a gingerbread party for a few friends. Put out the supplies and provide the houses and let your guests bring a snack or two to share and have a fun time together.

Try some of these fun items on your next gingerbread house.

Licorice Ropes	Candy Buttons
Peppermints	Sour Candy Belts
Gumdrops	M&Ms
Pretzels	Assorted Sprinkles
Colored Sugar	Chocolate Covered Sunflower Seeds
Royal Icing	Rainbow Colored Candy Discs
Ribbon Candy	Rock Candy
Mini Candy Canes	Candy Wafers
Cinnamon Imperials	Puffed Rice Treats

Day 11

Hope of the Season

Mary and Joseph as yet lived in their own separate homes in Nazareth in the northern province of Galilee at the time Gabriel told them of the Messiah she was to birth. The prophet Micah had foretold that Messiah would be born in Bethlehem in the southern kingdom of Judea. How was that to happen?

Luke 2:1-7 (NKJV)
1 And it came to pass in those days that a decree went out from Caesar Augustus that all the world should be registered. 2 This census first took place while Quirinius was governing Syria. 3 So all went to be registered, everyone to his own city. 4 Joseph also went up from Galilee, out of the city of Nazareth, into Judea, to the city of David, which is called Bethlehem, because he was of the house and lineage of David, 5 to be registered with Mary, his betrothed wife, who was with child. 6 So it was, that while they were there, the days were completed for her to be delivered. 7 And she brought forth her firstborn Son, and wrapped Him in swaddling cloths, and laid Him in a manger, because there was no room for them in the inn.

It was no more difficult for God to orchestrate the affairs of the emperor than of a carpenter. He could have spoken to Joseph in a dream as He had done previously, instructing him to travel with Mary to Bethlehem. Instead, He manipulated the plans of unwitting Augustus to fulfill His purpose. Perhaps Joseph was hoping Mary would give birth before the registration deadline, thereby perhaps exempting her from traveling. However, she did not, so they made that rugged trip of over 100 miles and large elevation changes with her being near delivery.

When we see the Christmas story in light of the big picture of redemption, it confirms for us God's infinite power and knowledge. Our mortal minds tend to focus on the temporal aspects of the story—the people, the places, the times. We are reminded that while God works in the context of such realms, He Himself transcends all aspects of creation, using them for His grand purposes. This season, may we celebrate His transcendent nature which He has exercised for our salvation.

Personal Reflections

_____

_____

_____

_____

_____

_____

_____

_____

Christmas Caroling

Caroling isn't done as much as it used to be, but that doesn't mean there aren't still folks out there that wouldn't love to hear a joyful noise! Gather a group together and pass out copies of a few of your favorite Christmas carols. Decide in advance which verses you are going to sing for each song. A day or two before you plan to go, call those you'd like to visit and make sure they'll be home and available. Is there someone like grandparents or elderly neighbors that would welcome some holiday cheer? Maybe a local nursing home that would enjoy the visit? Maybe a family with young kids that might be enraptured by opening their door to their very own personal choir presentation? Finish the night back at your central meeting spot with hot cocoa and cookies!

Day 12

Hope of the Season

Luke 2:8-18 (NIV2011)
⁸ And there were shepherds living out in the fields nearby, keeping watch over their flocks at night. ⁹ An angel of the Lord appeared to them, and the glory of the Lord shone around them, and they were terrified. ¹⁰ But the angel said to them, "Do not be afraid. I bring you good news that will cause great joy for all the people. ¹¹ Today in the town of David a Savior has been born to you; he is the Messiah, the Lord. ¹² This will be a sign to you: You will find a baby wrapped in cloths and lying in a manger." ¹³ Suddenly a great company of the heavenly host appeared with the angel, praising God and saying, ¹⁴ "Glory to God in the highest heaven, and on earth peace to those on whom his favor rests." ¹⁵ When the angels had left them and gone into heaven, the shepherds said to one another, "Let's go to Bethlehem and see this thing that has happened, which the Lord has told us about." ¹⁶ So they hurried off and found Mary and Joseph, and the baby, who was lying in the manger. ¹⁷ When they had seen him, they spread the word concerning what had been told them about this child, ¹⁸ and all who heard it were amazed at what the shepherds said to them.

Are we also amazed whenever we read this passage? Or does the familiarity of this story detract from the awe of it. Imagine the shepherds, the angels, the terror, the glory, the wonder. Think about *all who heard it were amazed.* Of course they were. This is not a fairy tale. This is historical reality. It was every bit as unique to them as it would be to you.

Let's go to Bethlehem and see this thing that has happened . . . The shepherds responded with genuine eager anticipation. May we be as eager to seize the Lord's presence. The angels came to them in their humble state. Shepherds were on the low end of the social scale in Palestine. Why did the angels come to them rather than to the movers and shakers of that society? God has always given grace to the humble. This Christmas, may we not be so full of ourselves, that we overlook the things of God right before our eyes. Lord, help our wayward hearts to recalculate; to put you in the center of our celebration. Jesus certainly had our need at the center of his zealous purpose. He would one day describe himself as the *good shepherd*, used in a divinely endearing way.

Personal Reflections

_____

_____

_____

_____

_____

_____

_____

_____

Paper Snowflakes

Remember paper snowflakes? Kids still love to make them!

1. Start with a square piece of paper.

2. Fold in half diagonally. (see diagram 1)

3. Fold in half again. (see diagram 2)

4. Fold that triangle into thirds and fold the right "third" over and then fold the left "third" over. (see diagram 3)

5. Cut the loose ends off as well as the tip. (see diagram 4).

6. Make any other cuts you'd like. Avoid cutting completely through from one side of the triangle to the other. (see diagram 5 for an example)

7. Gently open to reveal your snowflake.

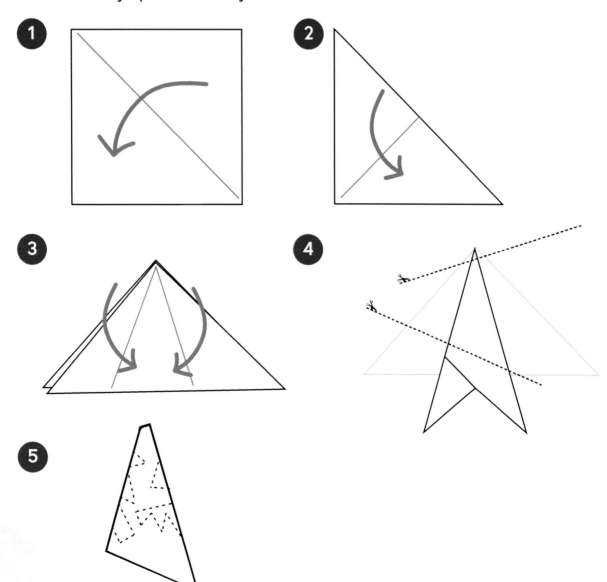

Day 13

Hope of the Season

Luke 2:6-7 (ESV)
⁶ And while they were there, the time came for her to give birth. ⁷ And she gave birth to her firstborn son and wrapped him in swaddling cloths and laid him in a manger, because there was no place for them in the inn.

No telling of the Christmas story would be complete without mentioning that Jesus first crib was a manger. Some have vilified the innkeeper for putting them in a stable. Others have suggested that the innkeeper was showing them kindness to give them some privacy away from the crowded inn. Whichever the case, it seems evident he knew nothing of the significance of the one being born. When the angels appeared to the shepherds to announce the divine birth, we read:

Luke 2:12 (ESV)
¹² And this will be a sign for you: you will find a baby wrapped in swaddling cloths and lying in a manger."

The swaddling cloths were not a sign. That would have been normal. The unique sign was where he laid his head—in a manger. This was not a detail that slipped through the crack when God planned this event. The manger silently testifies to the characteristic and purpose for Jesus' birth. The manger signifies his nature, that he was *meek and lowly and humble in heart*. It accordingly signifies that his methods of reigning at his incarnation would not be with political power, favor and influence. Rather, his kingdom would work within human hearts.

Our hearts are represented by the crowded inn. Do you have room for him? Do the eagerness of family, the buying and wrapping of presents, the decorating, and of celebrating the traditions of the season leave room for him to have a place of privacy there, a place of priority, of supremacy?

Personal Reflections

_____

_____

_____

_____

_____

_____

_____

_____

Coupons

If you are looking to cut the budget this year, or if you have a relative to whom you want to give something new and interesting, consider giving coupons for services. Fill out a coupon and wrap it up like a gift certificate and give it to your loved one. Make sure they know you intend to fulfill it and if they don't ask you about it, you'll be asking them!

Here are a few coupons you could consider giving to adults:

- Lawn mowing for a week/month
- Babysitting for an evening while the parents go out
- Cleaning/detailing a car
- Cleaning out a closet
- Pet sitting while out of town
- Bringing over a homemade dinner on a busy night
- Planting flowers in the Spring

Here are a few coupons you could consider giving to kids:

- Ice cream date
- Board game night together
- Movie Night
- "You pick the restaurant"
- Dollar Store run with $10 to spend
- Mom gives a manicure and pedicure
- Invite two friends to spend the night
- Cookie making and decorating day
- Trip to the library
- Bowling outing with the family

 Printables available in the back of this book.

Day 14

Hope of the Season

Nearly every nativity scene has a sheep or two in it. Sheep were present when the angels proclaimed Jesus' birth to the shepherds. Yet, they are always in the shadows. No notice is given to the sheep in the nativity narrative except to note the shepherds were keeping watch over them. Sheep were a source of income for the wool they produced. Because the fields around Bethlehem were so near Jerusalem, it is often speculated that these particular sheep were being raised to sell to Jews journeying to the temple, to be offered in a sacrificial ceremony.

Providentially, just as baby lambs were being born and raised for sacrifice, Jesus was also born in Bethlehem to be offered as a sacrifice at Jerusalem for the sins of the world.

Matthew 20:28 (ESV)
28 even as the Son of Man came not to be served but to serve, and to give his life as a ransom for many."

Jesus was called by John the Baptist, the Lamb of God. Jesus taught this analogy to his disciples before he died, but they did not understand until after he died and was resurrected. Jesus took upon himself this parallelism with sacrificial sheep. That equivalence is obscurely pictured by his birth in sheep country.

Personal Reflections

_____

_____

_____

_____

_____

_____

_____

_____

_____

_____

Want-Need-Wear-Read

It's hard not to spoil our loved ones at Christmas, but if you are looking for something to help keep your gift buying in check, here's an easy way to do it. Commit to buying your child, spouse, or loved one a total of four gifts:

- **Something you Want**
- **Something you Need**
- **Something to Wear**
- **Something to Read**

This helps you really focus on what you are buying and making it meaningful! Here are some examples for each category:

Something you want can be a big or small item, electronic device, Lego set, dollhouse, the "must have" toy item, the "wow" item!

Something you need can be something like a new sleeping bag, new backpack or luggage, new bedspread, a fun new lamp to replace an old one, etc. Just because they "need" it doesn't mean it has to be boring.

Something to Wear can be a new outfit, new pajamas, new coat, new shoes, but it can also be dress up clothes, new roller blades, a new hat, etc.

Something to Read can be a new book, a new series of books, cookbooks, magazine subscription, comic books, even a new Kindle or e-reader.

When doing this plan, you can add extra fun treats in a stocking or add a "family gift" (a board game, a new DVD, or a vacation!). The point isn't to be rigid, it's to be thoughtful about what you want to give to those you love.

Note: Another variation on this idea is the "three gift" policy. Every child in the family gets three gifts to honor the gifts of gold, frankincense, and myrrh that were brought to Jesus by the Wise Men.

Day 15

Hope of the Season

Eight days after Jesus' birth, Joseph and Mary took him to the temple in Jerusalem to be circumcised and for their purification after childbirth, according to Mosaic Law. As they entered the outer courts, they were confronted by Simeon.

Luke 2:25-35 (ESV)
²⁵ Now there was a man in Jerusalem, whose name was Simeon, and this man was righteous and devout, waiting for the consolation of Israel, and the Holy Spirit was upon him. ²⁶ And it had been revealed to him by the Holy Spirit that he would not see death before he had seen the Lord's Christ. ²⁷ And he came in the Spirit into the temple, and when the parents brought in the child Jesus, to do for him according to the custom of the Law, ²⁸ he took him up in his arms and blessed God and said, ²⁹ "Lord, now you are letting your servant depart in peace, according to your word; ³⁰ for my eyes have seen your salvation ³¹ that you have prepared in the presence of all peoples, ³² a light for revelation to the Gentiles, and for glory to your people Israel." ³³ And his father and his mother marveled at what was said about him. ³⁴ And Simeon blessed them and said to Mary his mother, "Behold, this child is appointed for the fall and rising of many in Israel, and for a sign that is opposed ³⁵ (and a sword will pierce through your own soul also), so that thoughts from many hearts may be revealed."

Simeon had received a prophetic message from the Lord, identifying Jesus as the long-awaited Messiah. His proclamation was not that for which the mainstream of Judaism was anticipating—a mighty warrior who would cast out Rome from their territory. Simeon seems to see the real purpose of Jesus' first coming; *a light for revelation to the Gentiles, and for glory to your people Israel.* He also foretold of Mary's anguish ahead. Then they encountered Anna.

Luke 2:36-38 (ESV)
³⁶ And there was a prophetess, Anna, the daughter of Phanuel, of the tribe of Asher. She was advanced in years, having lived with her husband seven years from when she was a virgin, ³⁷ and then as a widow until she was eighty-four. She did not depart from the temple, worshiping with fasting and prayer night and day. ³⁸ And coming up at that very hour she began to give thanks to God and to speak of him to all who were waiting for the redemption of Jerusalem.

Anna was spreading the news of Jesus to devout hopefuls in Jerusalem. We have way more information and clarity than she did then. How are we spreading the good news this Christmas?

Personal Reflections

_____
_____
_____
_____
_____
_____
_____
_____

Table Décor

For your holiday table, here are a few fun décor ideas:

- Put the silverware in a tiny stocking and put the stocking next to or on each plate.

- Use decorative paper straws to make any drink look festive.

- Use any of your clear kitchen bowls filled with your favorite ornaments as a centerpiece.

- Use a paint pen to put an initial or a name on a solid red ornament and set it on each plate as a place card.

- Mason jars filled with real cranberries are a festive centerpiece.

- A long table can have a green garland down the middle with ornaments or candles throughout it. That makes a long, low centerpiece that people can see each other over without having to move it.

- Google or look on Pinterest for some fun napkin folding ideas.

- Tie a jingle bell using a red ribbon onto the stem of your glasses if using stemware for your table.

- You can find printable Christmas scenes to print out and use as placemats for the "kids table." Tie a few crayons up with a ribbon put by each place setting and encourage drawing on the place mat or put brown or white butcher paper over the whole table and let the kids color all over it during and after the meal.

 Printables available in the back of this book.

Day 16

It seems that the star of Bethlehem is a major part of the Christmas story. It is commonly seen on Christmas cards, nativity sets, paintings and storybooks. It is usually depicted as a magnificent stellar phenomenon, lighting up the entire countryside and signaling to the world that something monumental was happening in Bethlehem that night. This makes a great story line. Is it biblical?

The magi were probably from the region of ancient Babylon. They were Gentiles, pagans, meaning they were not Jewish and that they originally did not know the God of Israel, the God of our Old Testament. The gospel of Matthew is the only place where we find anything written about the wise men or the star. It reads like this:

Matthew 2:1-2 (NKJV)
¹ Now after Jesus was born in Bethlehem of Judea in the days of Herod the king, behold, wise men from the East came to Jerusalem,
² saying, "Where is He who has been born King of the Jews? For we have seen His star in the East and have come to worship Him."

Besides the magi, who else saw the star? No one else is reported in the Bible as seeing it. If it had been a spectacular occurrence, surely everyone in the area would have seen it. Surely one of the New Testaments writers would have referred to it. It would seem that it was only seen and noted by the magi because they were stargazers, astrologers who kept careful track of the star patterns, whereas the Jews did not. It may well be that the star was not quite so prominent as we tend to think, if no one in Judea noticed it.

Thus, if this is so, it seems that the star was brought by God solely as a sign to the magi. He was calling these pagan stargazers to get acquainted with the God of Israel, the only true God. God was sending a witness to the nations outside Israel, even as Jesus was born. Past generations of pagans had experienced the God of Abraham, Isaac and Jacob in the past, but this new generation did not know of Him. That was about to change. These wise men would return home with an enlightened perspective of the God of the Hebrews. May this Christmas do that for each of us.

Personal Reflections

_____

_____

_____

_____

_____

_____

_____

_____

_____

Ornament Collections

An ornament collection can be a really special gift to start for yourself or for someone else! It's fun to purchase an ornament each year to add to the collection and watch it grow. With kids, you can purchase an ornament each year that represents an interest or hobby of theirs for that year or you can purchase a favorite character themed ornament. For a friend or relative, you might purchase a particular style or brand of ornament or a dated ornament year after year.   For yourself, you might purchase an ornament while on vacation or during any special travels or special events to serve as both a souvenir and Christmas decor.

Day 17

Hope of the Season

For many of us today, reading from the Christmas stories brings a warm and endearing message of familiarity. Yet, when you put yourself into the story, it was not all endearing. The story of the magi was marked by deceit, treachery and mania.

Matthew 2:1-3 (ESV)
¹ Now after Jesus was born in Bethlehem of Judea in the days of Herod the king, behold, wise men from the east came to Jerusalem, ² saying, "Where is he who has been born king of the Jews? For we saw his star when it rose and have come to worship him." ³ When Herod the king heard this, he was troubled, and all Jerusalem with him;

Why was all Jerusalem troubled along with Herod? It was because Herod was a mad man. When he was upset, heads would roll. He was motivated by extreme paranoia over the security of his kingship. This pronouncement of a new king ignited his vicious plan to kill this Messiah.

We see in this short story a cross-section of humanity in any age. We see the magi, outsiders, who traveled a very long journey to seek out the Messiah. At the opposite end of the spectrum we have a ferocious antagonist in Herod. In the populace of Jerusalem, we have a people who, all their lives, have paid homage to the Jewish expectation of a coming Messiah, who knew enough about the magi's visit and its effect on Herod to be troubled by it, yet did not make the four mile journey to Bethlehem to check it out. These are the indifferent.

With all the distractions at Christmas, it is easy to become complacent in our walk with the Lord. This Christmas, may we be among those who eagerly seek to encounter Jesus. For you and yours, may Christmas be, above all, a quest for a nearer presence of Jesus.

Personal Reflections

_____

_____

_____

_____

_____

_____

_____

Save the Christmas Cards

What do you do with the gorgeous Christmas cards you get in the mail during this season? Here are a few ideas:

•   Hang them on a ribbon with a clothes pin and drape the ribbon across a room or a mantle.

•   Take a picture of the photo on the cards and attach that photo to that person's name/number in your phone. That way when you text or call that person, their photo will show up.

•   Put the cards in a basket on your dining room table and take one out each night or each week and pray for that family.

•   Keep the cards and put them in a bag and pack them away with your decorations. Then the following year, you'll be able to pull them out, send cards to everyone from that pile before discarding them. Save the envelopes for easy access to their mailing addresses.

Day 18
Hope of the Season

By the time the magi arrived in Bethlehem, Jesus was no longer in the stable. He was living in a house and likely may have been about a year old, give or take a few months. These pagan noblemen of royal heritage and much prestige had traveled westward from *the east* about 1000 miles for several months to arrive at this moment. Then they did a most remarkable thing.

Matthew 2:11 (NKJV)
11 And when they had come into the house, they saw the young Child with Mary His mother, and fell down and worshiped Him. And when they had opened their treasures, they presented gifts to Him: gold, frankincense, and myrrh.

They were doing more than just showing royal courtesy or paying homage. They *worshiped* this little child. After all the signs God had given them, they were no longer just delegates. They were now on a pilgrimage of increasing intrigue. They discovered that the God of the Hebrews was personally calling them. And if He called them, would He not also accept their heartfelt, genuine worship?

These pagan noblemen humbled themselves before the child. Humility is the essential prerequisite for acceptable worship. Many passages in scripture teach us that God *resists the proud, but gives grace to the humble*. Whenever we approach God, whether in worship, study, meditation or in prayer, we must recognize that it is only because of His great mercy that we are welcomed into His presence. We must further understand that we are made welcome by the atoning sacrifice of Jesus. This is the good news of Christmas.

Personal Reflections

_____

_____

_____

_____

_____

_____

_____

Nativity Scene

A nativity scene can be a special and tangible way to honor the Savior throughout the season. For young kids, there are plastic or cloth sets you can use. For older kids, the resin or ceramic sets are special. Make a special tradition of putting the set up together or having kids take turns putting baby Jesus in the manger. Some families like to put the wise men on a different table and move them closer to the manger each day to represent that they saw the star and started their journey.

Day 19

Matthew 2:11 (NKJV)
¹¹ And when they had come into the house, they saw the young Child with Mary His mother, and fell down and worshiped Him. And when they had opened their treasures, they presented gifts to Him: gold, frankincense, and myrrh.

Their gifts were appropriate for a king, a priest and a burial. The magi were likely from the land of ancient Babylon. They were astrologers, believing that the stars signaled new kings and kingdoms. In the Old Testament book of Daniel, we see that the exiled Jew Daniel prophesied from God-given wisdom and revelation which resulted in him being made head over all the wise men of Babylon, *the magicians [hence the title magi], the enchanters, the sorcerers and the Chaldeans.* This group of wise men had survived several changes of dynasty and still existed in Jesus' day.

The magi would have possessed both the legacy of Daniel and the ancient Hebrew scripture scrolls confiscated during the exile period. In preparing for their journey, the magi likely researched these scriptures (Our Old Testament) and discovered the many prophetic promises about Messiah. In doing so, they likely also found three prophesied messianic portraits: King of kings, great high priest and suffering servant. The parallel symbolism between the portraits and the magi's gifts is difficult to dismiss. It seems reasonable that their gifts were intentionally selected, albeit with divine guidance, to fit those portrayed roles of Messiah. At Christmas, we welcome him as our king, our great high priest and as our atoning sacrifice.

Personal Reflections

Ornament Exchange

Whether it's an office party or a kids' classroom get together, an ornament exchange can be a fun activity. It's inexpensive and easy. Everyone brings a wrapped Christmas ornament and you can decide ahead of time if you want it to be silly or serious (or just let people decide for themselves). You can draw numbers and let each person go in order and choose an ornament to unwrap and keep or you can play a game where the first person opens it and then the next person can either steal that one or choose a new one. Set a limit of how many times an ornament can be stolen (2-3 times) before it's frozen. If playing with kids, suggest ornaments that can't easily be broken in the excitement of the game.

Day 20

It is likely that as the magi prepared to journey to Israel, their research uncovered this ancient prophecy of Balaam,

Numbers 24:17 (ESV)
17 I see him, but not now; I behold him, but not near: a star shall come out of Jacob, and a scepter shall rise out of Israel; it shall crush the forehead of Moab and break down all the sons of Sheth.

This prophecy is unique and remarkable in that Balaam was not Jewish, not Hebrew. He was a Gentile (non-Jewish) 'prophet.' Although he was Gentile, God spoke through him, controlling his words and message. The passage seems out of place in a cursory reading of the context in which it was given. So, why was its message given? Perhaps its message was for a future generation. If the magi, 1500 years later, did read it, think about this.

Here we have in Hebrew scripture a Gentile prophet speaking to Gentile magi about a Jewish Messiah. Perhaps it propelled them as they then discovered and pondered the multiple other Jewish messianic prophecies. Since the magi were stargazers, and since their culture believed that the stars somehow told of the rising of kings, they would have easily equated this prophecy to an actual star like the one they had seen.

God worked through their culture of stargazing to reach them. We see a most magnanimous God crossing cultural barriers to reach a people far away. Think how much providential coordination took place to make the visit of the magi happen. God is a seeking God, a revealing God. Christmas is a time of revealing.

Personal Reflections

_____

_____

_____

_____

_____

_____

_____

_____

_____

Place Cards

We love to use place cards for Christmas Day or for holiday gatherings. You or the kids can make them using cardstock and stickers, paint pens on ornaments, or anything they can dream up. If the place card is accompanied by a piece of candy or small gift, even better. If kids are especially creative, they could draw a picture on each one or a picture of the person the place card is for! Set the place cards by the glasses at each place setting and take away the confusion of who is sitting where, plus everyone feels special to see their name at their spot.

 Printables available in the back of this book.

Day 21

Hope of the Season

Matthew 2:7-8,12-15 (NKJV)

7 Then Herod, when he had secretly called the wise men, determined from them what time the star appeared. 8 And he sent them to Bethlehem and said, "Go and search carefully for the young Child, and when you have found Him, bring back word to me, that I may come and worship Him also."

Herod's diabolical intention was to kill this challenger for his throne.

12 Then, being divinely warned in a dream that they [the wise men] should not return to Herod, they departed for their own country another way. 13 Now when they had departed, behold, an angel of the Lord appeared to Joseph in a dream, saying, "Arise, take the young Child and His mother, flee to Egypt, and stay there until I bring you word; for Herod will seek the young Child to destroy Him." 14 When he arose, he took the young Child and His mother by night and departed for Egypt, 15 and was there until the death of Herod, that it might be fulfilled which was spoken by the Lord through the prophet, saying, "Out of Egypt I called My Son."

Note the urgency. They began their travel in the middle of the night. This was no casual stroll. My wife Chery and I once made the trip from Jerusalem to Cairo by tour bus. We started at about 8:00 AM and arrived after dark. I'm sure our rout was quite different from the rout this little family took; nevertheless, it was a grueling journey for them by foot through arid terrain, requiring many days of travel. When Herod realized his plans had been foiled, he gave orders to kill all boys under two years of age in Bethlehem, thus eliminating any competition for his throne. This is how we draw a rough idea as to how old Jesus was when the magi visited him. The wise men were oblivious to Herod's plan until God warned them in a dream.

This might raise the question, 'Since God was protecting Jesus from destruction, why did he require such hardship of them? Herod was the bad guy here. Why didn't God just take him out?' We can't answer that from our limited logical vantage point. However, we are told something very revealing. *"Out of Egypt I called My Son."* Even though we cannot understand, we can recognize that there was purpose in this plan. The purpose even warranted a prophetic prediction of it. We trust God was working things according to His plan. God was not the author of the evil in Herod's heart, but His plans accommodated the existence of evil for a season, for a reason. Such are much of our lives. As did Joseph and Mary, so should we simply trust and obey.

Personal Reflections

_____

_____

_____

_____

_____

_____

Extra Gifts

Sometimes during the season, you meet up with friends for lunch or have someone drop by the house and you wish you had a gift you could give. Or you may have a last minute invitation and want to take a hostess gift. It's never a bad idea to purchase a few gifts during the season to have on hand to give and be a blessing! For adults, here are a few ideas of gifts that you might pick up during the season: gift card for coffee inside an insulated mug, a warm fuzzy scarf, a handful of new kitchen utensils, a pair of earrings that you love, a favorite book you enjoyed reading this year, etc. For the kiddos in your life: a puzzle, board game, art supplies, Target gift card, or a stuffed animal are all fun items.

If you end up with extra gifts at the end of the season, you can save them to give for upcoming birthdays or you can donate them.

Day 22

Hope of the Season

Hebrews 1:1-2 (ESV)
¹ Long ago, at many times and in many ways, God spoke to our fathers by the prophets, ² but in these last days he has spoken to us by his Son, whom he appointed the heir of all things, through whom also he created the world.

At Christmas, we behold a lot more than a baby in a manger. Jesus was God's consummate self-revelation to man. In the past, God had revealed Himself to certain people in prophetic dreams and visions, special encounters and symbolic worship practices. They saw shadows of Him. At Christmas, He entered our world as one of us. He revealed Himself to us more personally. In Jesus' incarnation, he emptied himself of the outward attributes of his glory so that we could approach him in intimate nearness. He revealed his glory indirectly, with increasing immensity, through his words and works.

Some of his works were done before crowds. Some were performed only before the twelve apostles, or an even smaller group of them. But on the night of his betrayal, he prayed a long prayer in the presence of his apostles in which he said this:

John 17:20-21 (ESV)
²⁰ "I do not ask for these only [the twelve], but also for those who will believe in me through their word, ²¹ that they may all be one, just as you, Father, are in me, and I in you, that they also may be in us, so that the world may believe that you have sent me.

God is revealing Himself, through Jesus, to us who believe. He is inviting a relationship with us based on our embrace of his Lordship. He draws us to himself that we might have eternal life. Give Him thanks for being a revealing and seeking God. Oh, rejoice in the very revelation of God in that manger.

Personal Reflections

_____

_____

_____

_____

_____

_____

_____

_____

_____

_____

_____

Christmas Photos to Take

There are always lots of pictures being taken this season, but here are a few to remember to take:

- Making cookies or Christmas crafts
- Wrapping Christmas gifts
- Kissing under the mistletoe
- Wearing Christmas pajamas
- In the church lobby before the Christmas Eve service
- Holding your annual Christmas card
- Photos of any Christmas traditions
- An annual picture that you re-create each year
- Kids holding their Christmas wish lists
- Decorating the tree
- A photo of every guest at your Christmas Day celebration
- A photo of the person that usually takes all the pictures

Day 23

Philippians 2:5-11 (ESV)
⁵ Have this mind among yourselves, which is yours in Christ Jesus, ⁶ who, though he was in the form of God, did not count equality with God a thing to be grasped, ⁷ but emptied himself, by taking the form of a servant, being born in the likeness of men. ⁸ And being found in human form, he humbled himself by becoming obedient to the point of death, even death on a cross. ⁹ Therefore God has highly exalted him and bestowed on him the name that is above every name, ¹⁰ so that at the name of Jesus every knee should bow, in heaven and on earth and under the earth, ¹¹ and every tongue confess that Jesus Christ is Lord, to the glory of God the Father.

Here Paul summarizes Jesus' incarnation in a few sweeping sentences. Jesus, the second member of the Trinity, did not come into existence on that first Christmas. He had always existed with the Father and the Spirit, and now is temporarily taking on human mortality, flesh and blood. This is consistent with what John taught in his profound 'nativity' statement in which he calls Jesus the *Word*.

John 1:1-2,14 (ESV)
¹ In the beginning was the Word, and the Word was with God, and the Word was God. ² He was in the beginning with God. . . ¹⁴ And the Word became flesh and dwelt among us, and we have seen his glory, glory as of the only Son from the Father, full of grace and truth.

God came in the person of Jesus to save us from our sins. This great God, Father Almighty, Creator, Lord and Sovereign, came to suffer and die. When we celebrate Jesus' birth, we are celebrating the initiation of the pivot point in redemptive history. He certainly deserves our celebration and worship, both because of His essential worthiness and because of His saving initiative. May the joy of our festivities this Christmas be about Him.

Personal Reflections

_____

_____

_____

_____

_____

_____

_____

Night Before Christmas Box

Consider a fun tradition called the "Night Before Christmas Box." It's a box that is to be opened each year on Christmas Eve and may contain Christmas pajamas, Christmas socks, a Christmas movie, popcorn, candy, cookie mix, a board game, a puzzle, packets of hot cocoa, a book to read, the Christmas story typed out or a small Bible, etc. Choose the things your family would enjoy doing and you can change it up every year if you'd like. The whole family gathers to open the box together and looks forward to the night ahead!

Photocopy these sample tags below and use for your boxes.

Day 24

Hope of the Season

Angels are often a prominent theme at Christmas. We hang them on Christmas trees or set them as table decorations. Christmas cards show them surrounding the events of Christmas. Often they are depicted as infant children with wings, but in fact they are powerful beings. Sometimes they are depicted as women, but in scripture they are always spoken of in the masculine gender. They are repeatedly involved in the Christmas narratives in the Bible. The angel Gabriel spoke to Zechariah, father of John the Baptist, then to Mary. An angel appeared to the shepherds, followed by a host of the heavenly beings, praising God. The glory of heaven shown about them.

Angels were the most visibly splendored beings in the nativity narratives, but as glorious as they were, they were never the focus of the story. They were God's messengers. We should not give praise to them. They are always proclaiming Jesus as the One to be praised and worshipped.

The book of Hebrews opens with a litany of comparisons showing the superiority of Jesus over the angels. Angels are created beings, whereas, Jesus is eternal. Angels are servants, while Jesus is the Son. What is their role, their purpose? One main role is revealed in that passage.

Hebrews 1:14 (ESV)
¹⁴ Are they [angels] not all ministering spirits sent out to serve for the sake of those who are to inherit salvation?

Remember, it is people who are made in the image of God. Although we are flawed and weak compared to angels, nevertheless, we who trust in Jesus as Lord are ordained to eternal life in the family of God. What a mind-blowing thought! What a glorious destiny we have! At Christmas, the angels remind us of our upward call. In the midst of our planning, decorating and bustling around, may we not fail to focus on things above this Christmas, and afterward. The reason for the season, the treasure of the pleasure, the joys beyond the toys, the love of God for each of us as reflected in our love for family in togetherness –may it all point us to the divine purpose.

Personal Reflections

_____

_____

_____

_____

_____

_____

_____

Candlelight Service

Many churches have a candlelight service on Christmas Eve. Some have several time options including late afternoon options for family with young kids, evening options for anyone, and even midnight options for those that want to see Christmas officially start as the service ends. Find a local church with a service time that works for you and come prepared to sing carols, hear the Christmas story, and light candles together. If you are worried about your child holding a candle, you can bring a glow stick (from the dollar store). If you are not in your home town for Christmas, you are sure to find a church to welcome you by asking a friend or relative from the area where you are spending the holiday or searching the internet.

If you aren't able to get out for a service or prefer to stay in, you can have your own candlelight service. Find a few candles around the house to use. Then read the Christmas story from the Bible, have participants share their favorite Christmas memories or reflective thoughts, sing some Christmas carols (Silent Night, O Holy Night, Angels we Have Heard on High). At the end, turn off the lights and light your candles.

Day 25

Paul used the phrase *'fullness of time'* twice to emphasize the perfection of God's timing. His first use refers to the timing of Jesus' incarnation.

Galatians 4:4 (ESV)
⁴ But when the fullness of time had come, God sent forth his Son, born of woman, born under the law,

We often do not understand His timing. We grow impatient to see answers to our prayers and fulfillment of God's promises. The scripture says Jesus was born at just the right time.

In Paul's second use of the term, he is referring to the consummation of all things at the end of the age. God withheld information from Jesus' disciples, even from Jesus himself, regarding the timing of end-of-the-age events. It was not for them to know.

Ephesians 1:7-10 (ESV)
⁷ In him we have redemption through his blood, the forgiveness of our trespasses, according to the riches of his grace, ⁸ which he lavished upon us, in all wisdom and insight ⁹ making known to us the mystery of his will, according to his purpose, which he set forth in Christ ¹⁰ as a plan for the fullness of time, to unite all things in him, things in heaven and things on earth.

According to Paul's second use of the fullness of time, He is making known to Christians the mystery of His purpose to unite all things in him, but not the timing of it. We are taught in scripture to anticipate, to watch, to cherish, to trust, but not to speculate on the timing. Are you ready and anxious to meet Jesus at his return? He wants to be your delight, not your fear, when he comes again.

Personal Reflections

_____

_____

_____

_____

_____

_____

_____

The Real Christmas Story

Every Christmas Eve or Christmas morning, make a tradition of reading the Christmas story from the Bible. Older kids can do the reading out loud to the family or younger kids can listen while parents or older siblings read.

Read Luke 2:1-20 (see below) or if you have the Bible app on your phone, you can curl up together and listen to that. Just look for a bible app version that has an audio option.

LUKE 2: 1-20

CHRIST BORN OF MARY
And it came to pass in those days that a decree went out from Caesar Augustus that all the world should be registered. 2 This census first took place while Quirinius was governing Syria. 3 So all went to be registered, everyone to his own city.

4 Joseph also went up from Galilee, out of the city of Nazareth, into Judea, to the city of David, which is called Bethlehem, because he was of the house and lineage of David, 5 to be registered with Mary, his betrothed [a] wife, who was with child. 6 So it was, that while they were there, the days were completed for her to be delivered. 7 And she brought forth her firstborn Son, and wrapped Him in swaddling cloths, and laid Him in a [b]manger, because there was no room for them in the inn.

GLORY IN THE HIGHEST
8 Now there were in the same country shepherds living out in the fields, keeping watch over their flock by night. 9 And [c] behold, an angel of the Lord stood before them, and the glory of the Lord shone around them, and they were greatly afraid. 10 Then the angel said to them, "Do not be afraid, for behold, I bring you good tidings of great joy which will be to all

people. 11 For there is born to you this day in the city of David a Savior, who is Christ the Lord. 12 And this will be the sign to you: You will find a Babe wrapped in swaddling cloths, lying in a [d]manger."

13 And suddenly there was with the angel a multitude of the heavenly host praising God and saying:

14

*"Glory to God in the highest,
And on earth peace,
goodwill[e] toward men!"*

15 So it was, when the angels had gone away from them into heaven, that the shepherds said to one another, "Let us now go to Bethlehem and see this thing that has come to pass, which the Lord has made known to us." 16 And they came with haste and found Mary and Joseph, and the Babe lying in a manger. 17 Now when they had seen Him, they made [f]widely known the saying which was told them concerning this Child. 18 And all those who heard it marveled at those things which were told them by the shepherds. 19 But Mary kept all these things and pondered them in her heart. 20 Then the shepherds returned, glorifying and praising God for all the things that they had heard and seen, as it was told them.

Holiday Recipes Index

Appetizers, Beverages & Snacks
Coffee Punch
Party Pizzas
Chex Mix
Nieman Marcus Dip
Brie and Cherry Pastry Cups

Salads, Sauces, & Soups
Glazed Fruit Salad
Balsamic Berry Vinaigrette Winter Salad
Cranberry Sauce
Butternut Squash Soup
White Chili

Side & Main Dishes
Breakfast Cinnamon Rolls
Sausage and Egg Casserole
Garlic Mushrooms with Bacon
Green Bean Bundles
Whipped Sweet Potato Bake
Broccoli and Cheese Casserole
Potato Casserole
Hot Curried Fruit

Desserts
Shortbread Cookies
Apple Dip
Candied Pecans
White Chocolate Popcorn
Creamy Pralines
Banana Nut Bread
Chocolate Éclair Cake

Coffee Punch

Ingredients:

8 cups boiling water
1 cup instant decaf coffee
    (Sanka or Nescafe)

¾ cup sugar
½ gallon vanilla ice cream
Cool whip (optional)

Directions:

Combine the boiling water, instant coffee and sugar the night before serving the punch. The next day, add the ice cream and cool whip, if desired.

Party Pizzas

Ingredients:

2 pounds of pork sausage (one pound
    hot and one pound mild, if desired)
1 pound Velveeta cheese
2 teaspoons A1 sauce
1 tablespoon ketchup

1 teaspoon oregano
Jar of salsa (any kind)
Party sized rye or wheat bread,
    usually found in the deli section

Directions:

Lay bread pieces on cookie sheet. Mix cooked sausage, softened cheese, A1 sauce, ketchup, and oregano together. Scoop mixture onto bread slices and flatten a little with the back of a spoon.

Spoon on a small bit of salsa on each slice and top with grated parmesan cheese, if desired. Cook for 10 minutes at 425 degrees.

Chex Mix

Ingredients:

- 1 cup mixed nuts
- 1 cup pretzels
- 1 cup cheerios
- 3 cups Corn Chex cereal
- 3 cups Wheat Chex cereal
- 3 cups Rice Chex cereal

- 6 tablespoons butter
- 2 tablespoons Worcestershire sauce
- ¾ teaspoon garlic powder
- 1 ½ teaspoon seasoned salt
- ½ teaspoon onion powder

Directions:

Heat oven to 250 degrees. Melt margarine in large roasting pan in oven. Stir in seasons. Gradually stir in remaining ingredients until evenly coated. Bake one hour, stirring every 15 minutes. Spread on paper towels to cool. Store in airtight container.

Nieman Marcus Dip

Ingredients:

- 6 green onions, chopped
- 8 ounces of cheddar cheese, shredded

- 1 ½ cups of mayonnaise
- 1 jar Hormel reach bacon bits
- 1 package slivered almonds

Directions:

Mix everything together and chill for a couple of hours. Serve with Ritz crackers (my favorite) or corn chips.

RECIPES

Brie and Cherry Pastry Cups

Ingredients:

1 sheet frozen puff pastry, thawed
½ cup red cherry preserves or a can
of cherry pie filling
4 ounces Brie cheese, cut into ½ x ½

inch pieces (36 pieces)
¼ cup chopped pecans
2 tablespoons fresh chives (optional)

Directions:

Heat oven to 375 degrees. Spray 36 mini muffin cups with cooking spray. Cut pastry into 36 squares (each will be 1.5 inches). Slightly press each square into muffin cup and press center with finger.

Bake 10 minutes. Press the center with the handle of a wooden spoon. Bake 6 to 8 minutes longer or until golden brown. Immediately press again in the center. Fill each with about ½ teaspoon preserves or one cherry from the pie filling. Top with piece of brie, pecans, and chives.

Bake 3 to 5 minutes or until the cheese is melted. Serve warm.

Glazed Fruit Salad

Ingredients:
- 1 package vanilla pudding (not instant)
- 1 package Americana tapioca pudding
- 1 large can pineapple tidbits, drained but save the juice
- 2 cans mandarin oranges, well drained
- 1 small jar maraschino cherries
- 3-5 sliced bananas
- ¾ cup chopped pecans (optional)

Directions:
Dissolve pudding mixes with the juice from the pineapple tidbits and enough water to make 2 cups of liquid. Bring to a boil and set aside to cool. Mix all of the fruit, making sure it is drained well. Right before serving add the cooled pudding mix, fruit, pecans, and sliced bananas together and stir.

Balsamic Berry Vinaigrette Winter Salad

Ingredients:
- ¼ c. balsamic vinegar
- 2 tablespoons plain Greek yogurt
- 1 tablespoon strawberry preserves
- 1 ½ teaspoon olive oil
- 1 teaspoon Dijon mustard
- 1 clove garlic, minced
- ¼ teaspoon kosher salt
- ⅛ teaspoon black pepper
- 3 cups fresh baby spinach
- 3 cups torn romaine lettuce
- 1 small cooking apple (gala), thinly sliced
- ½ c. crumbled feta or goat cheese (I use mozzarella because I'm boring)
- ½ cup pomegranate seeds
- ¼ cup chopped walnuts, toasted

Directions:
For the vinaigrette, in a small bowl whisk together vinegar, yogurt, preserves, oil, mustard, garlic, salt, and pepper

In an extra-large serving bowl, combine spinach, romaine, apple, cheese, pomegranate seeds, and walnuts. Drizzle with half of the dressing, toss to coat.

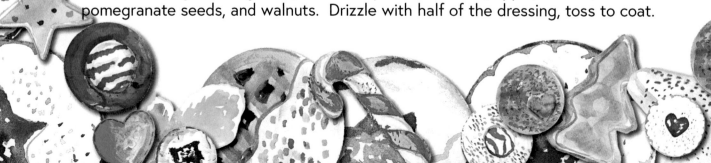

Cranberry Sauce

Ingredients:

1 bag of cranberries (12 oz. bag)
1 cup cranberry or apple juice

1 cup pure maple syrup
(not pancake syrup)
3 tablespoons orange juice
or orange zest

Directions:

Wash bag of cranberries and put in a medium saucepan. Pour in one cup of cranberry or apple juice and one cup of maple syrup. Add orange juice or zest. Stir together and turn heat on high until it reaches a boil. Once it comes to a rolling boil, turn the heat down to medium low and continue cooking for about ten minutes or until the juice is thick. Turn off the heat.

White Chili

Ingredients:

1 can of Navy Beans, undrained
1 can Great Northern Beans
1 can rotel tomatoes with green chilis
½ teaspoon cumin
2 teaspoon chili powder
⅜ teaspoon garlic powder

¼ teaspoon thyme
¾ cups cheddar cheese, shredded
¾ cups Monterey Jack cheese,
shredded
2 cans of chicken (or 2-3 cooked
chicken breasts, chopped)

Directions:

In a large pot, put the Navy beans, Great Northern beans, and can of rotel. Then add the cumin, chili powder, garlic powder, and thyme. Next add the chicken and cook for about 45 minutes. Then add the cheeses and cook an additional 15 minutes.

Butternut Squash Soup

Ingredients:

1 Tablespoon olive oil
1 onion, chopped
1 medium butternut squash, peeled and chopped
2 clove garlic, minced

6 c. hot chicken stock
1 teaspoon chopped fresh thyme
1 teaspoon chopped fresh sage
½ cup heavy cream
Salt and pepper

Ingredients for topping:

¼ c. heavy cream

¼ cup sour cream

Directions:

For the soup: Heat the olive oil in a large pot over medium high heat. Add the onion and cook until beginning to soften, about five minutes. Add the squash and cook, stirring occasionally, until beginning to brown around the edges, 8 to 10 minutes. Add the garlic and cook for another minute. Pour in the chicken stock, add the thyme and sage and bring to a simmer. Simmer until the squash is very soft, 10 to 15 minutes. Stir in the heavy cream. Puree using an immersion blender. Season with salt and pepper. Serve immediately or let cool completely and freeze.

For the topping, when ready to serve, mix together the cream and sour cream in a small bowl and drizzle over the soup. Add pine nuts or almonds, if desired.

Breakfast Cinnamon Rolls

Ingredients:

2 sticks of butter
½ cup brown sugar
1 c. chopped pecans

2 Tablespoons of cinnamon
1 c. sugar
18 frozen self-rising rolls

Directions:

Melt one stick of butter in a bundt pan. Add brown sugar and pecans. Mix cinnamon and sugar in a bowl. Melt one stick of butter. Take frozen rolls and dip them in butter and roll in the sugar mixture. Lay in pan. Add remaining butter and sugar. Let rise 6-8 hours or overnight. Bake at 300 degrees for 40-45 minutes.

Sausage and Egg Casserole

Ingredients:

1 pound sausage
6 slices of bread
2 cups milk
6 eggs, beaten

1 cup shredded cheese
  (cheddar or Colby jack)
1 teaspoon dry mustard
1 teaspoon salt
1 teaspoon oregano

Directions:

Brown and crumble sausage. Tear bread into pieces. Beat eggs and add milk. Add cheese, mustard, salt, and oregano. Put bread in bottom of 9x13 glass baking dish. Mix sausage with milk mixture. Pour over bread. Refrigerate 24 hours or overnight.

Remove from refrigerator when ready to cook and bake at 350 degrees for 45 to 60 minutes.

Garlic Mushrooms with Bacon

Ingredients:

24 medium white mushrooms
½ pound bacon
1 small onion, diced
6 garlic cloves, finely chopped

2 tablespoons of unsalted butter
Kosher salt and ground black pepper

Directions:

Quarter the mushrooms, cut in the bacon into thin strips and set aside. Melt the butter in a medium saute pan. Add the onions and garlic and cook for two minutes. Toss in the mushrooms and bacon and mix well. Season with salt and pepper and cook until the mushrooms and bacon are cooked through. Serve in small bowls alongside fresh crusty bread.

Green Bean Bundles

Ingredients:

3 cans whole green beans, drained
1 pound bacon, cut in half
½ cup butter, melted

1 cup brown sugar
1 teaspoon garlic salt

Directions:

Preheat oven to 350 degrees F. Grease a 9x13 inch baking dish. Wrap 7 green beans with bacon and place in prepared dish and repeat using all green beans and bacon. Combine butter with brown sugar and pour over the green bean bundles and sprinkle with garlic salt. Cover with foil and bake for 45 minutes.

Whipped Sweet Potato Bake

Ingredients:

3 cans (15 oz. each) Sweet potatoes, drained
¼ c. butter, melted
1 teaspoon ground cinnamon
½ tsp. salt

¼ teaspoon ground nutmeg
3 cups mini marshmallows
¼ cup brown sugar
Options, sprinkle of pecan pieces

Directions:

Preheat oven to 350 degrees F. Beat sweet potatoes, butter, cinnamon, sugar, brown sugar, nutmeg in medium bowl with electric mixer until well blended. Spoon into lightly greased 1.5-quart baking dish. Top with marshmallows and pecans, if desired.

Bake 15-20 minutes or until sweet potatoes are heated through and marshmallows are slightly browned.

Broccoli and Cheese Casserole

Ingredients:

Frozen chopped broccoli
1 small jar cheese whiz
1 can cream of chicken soup

2 tablespoons of butter
¾ cup minute rice

Directions:

Cook broccoli to package instructions. Add cheese whiz, soup, butter, and rice. Stir and pour into casserole dish. Sprinkle with paprika if desired. Bake at 350 degrees for 25 minutes.

Potato Casserole

Ingredients:

2-pound bag of frozen hash browns
¼ cup chopped onion
1 cup cream of chicken soup
¼ cup melted butter

1 teaspoon salt
¼ teaspoon pepper
1 cup sour cream
2 cups shredded cheddar cheese

Directions:

Combine items. Place in greased 9x13 baking dish. In a separate dish, melt ¼ c. butter and mix with 2 slices of bread, torn into pieces. Put the coated bread pieces on top of casserole and then bake at 350 degrees for 45-60 minutes.

Hot Curried Fruit

Ingredients:

Pear Halves
Peach or apricot halves
3 cups pineapple tidbits
1 small bottle maraschino cherries

⅓ cup melted butter
⅔ cup brown sugar
3 ½ teaspoon curry powder
3 tablespoons corn starch

Directions:

Drain fruit thoroughly and place hollow side up in a shallow two-quart casserole dish. Melt butter and add sugar, curry powder, and cornstarch. Pour over fruit. Bake at 325 degrees for one hour. This can be made a day in advance and reheated at 350 degrees for 30 minutes.

Shortbread Cookies

Ingredients:

½ cup unsalted butter
⅓ cup caster sugar (or blend regular
   sugar in blender to make extra fine)

1 cup plain flour, sifted
½ cup rice flour

Directions:

Preheat the oven to 300 degrees F. Lightly butter a 9-inch square pan or baking dish. Cream the butter and sugar together in a large bowl. Add the flour and rice flour and use a wooden spoon to work all ingredients together to make a paste. Knead lightly.

Press the mixture into the dish or tin, using the back of a spoon to smooth down the surface. Use a table knife to draw a line down the middle vertically, then mark six lines across horizontally to make 14 fingers. Prick each one with a fork.

Bake for about 30 minutes, then remove from the oven and mark again. Return to the oven and continue to bake for 30 minutes until the mixture is set.

Mark the 14 fingers again then sprinkle with a light dusting of sugar. Cool in the dish for about 30 minutes, then cut into pieces and carefully easy out of the pan. Finish cooling the shortbread on a wire rack then store in an airtight container.

Apple Dip

Ingredients:

8 oz. cream cheese, softened
½ cup brown sugar

½ cup granulated sugar
1 tsp. vanilla
5 oz. toffee bits (half a bag)

Directions:

Mix together all ingredients except the toffee and refrigerate. Add toffee bits in before serving. Sprinkle toffee bits on top for presentation. Serve with graham crackers, vanilla wafers, or fruit.

Candied Pecans

Ingredients:

1 large egg white
½ cup sugar
1 teaspoon freshly ground nutmeg

1 teaspoon ground cinnamon
½ teaspoon salt
2 cups pecan halves (8-9 ounces)

Directions:

Preheat oven to 300 degrees F. Brush large rimmed baking sheet with butter. Whisk egg white in bowl until foamy. Add sugar, spices, and salt. Whisk until mixture is thick and opaque. Add pecans; stir until coated. Using forks, transfer nuts to sheet, spacing apart; discard remaining coating.

Bake nuts until deep golden brown, about 35 minutes. Cool completely on sheet. Transfer to container. Cover and store at room temperature. Can be made 4 days ahead.

White Chocolate Popcorn

Ingredients:

6 ounces of White Chocolate Chips
2 (3 ⅓ ounce) bags of unbuttered Popcorn

Red and green M&M candies or mini M&M candies, optional

Directions:

Melt the chocolate in the microwave, watching closely that it doesn't burn. Microwave two bags of popcorn or pop about 7 ounces of popcorn kernels.

In a large tub or bowl, drizzle melted chocolate over the popcorn. Mix and fluff as you go. You are looking for a light coat of chocolate on the popcorn. Too much will make the popcorn soggy.

Let the popcorn cool in the refrigerator until the chocolate hardens. Add M&M candies if you want a pop of color and a little flavor of milk chocolate or enjoy as it is.

Creamy Pralines

Ingredients:

- 1 cup brown sugar
- 1 cup sugar
- 1 cup buttermilk
- ¾ teaspoon baking soda
- ½ teaspoon salt
- 1 ½ cups chopped pecans
- 2 tablespoons butter

Directions:

In a deep, large saucepan, place brown sugar, sugar, buttermilk, baking soda, and salt. Mix well and bring to a boil over medium heat, stirring constantly. Continue cooking until the mixture reaches 210 degrees on a candy thermometer.

Add the pecans and butter and continue cooking until thermometer reaches 230 degrees. Remove from heat and cool for two minutes. Beat with electric mixer about 3 minutes or until mixture is thick and starts to lose its shine. Do not overbeat. Dip by spoonfuls onto wax paper. Add a teaspoon of hot water if candy becomes too hard. Makes 24 pralines.

Banana Nut Bread

Ingredients:

- ¾ cup butter
- 1 ½ cups sugar
- ⅕ cups mashed bananas (3 medium)
- 2 eggs, well beaten
- 1 teaspoon vanilla
- 2 cups flour
- 1 teaspoon soda
- ¾ teaspoon salt
- ½ cup buttermilk
- ¾ cup walnuts, chopped

Directions:

Cream butter and sugar thoroughly. Blend in bananas, eggs and vanilla. Sift flour, baking soda, and salt together. Add to the banana mixture, alternating with buttermilk, mixing thoroughly after each addition. Add nuts, mix. Pour batter into greased and floured 9x5x3 inch loaf pan. Bake at 325 degrees for 1 ¼ hours or until done.

Chocolate Éclair Cake

Ingredients:

1 box of graham crackers
2 small packages of vanilla instant pudding

3 cups milk
1 can of chocolate frosting
1 8-oz tub of Cool Whip

Directions:
Make pudding with only 3 cups of milk. Fold into Cool Whip. Layer bottom of a 9 x 13 pan with graham crackers. Top with ½ pudding mixture. Add another layer of graham crackers and then another layer of pudding mixture. Finally, top with another layer of graham crackers.

Microwave the tub of chocolate frosting until pourable and pour it evenly over the pan for a smooth look. Best if made the night before so the crackers get soft.

Christmas Eve Menu

APPETIZER	
MAIN DISH	
SIDE ITEMS	
DESSERTS	
BEVERAGES	
OTHER	

Christmas Morning Menu

BEVERAGES	
SAVORY	
SWEET	
KID FRIENDLY	
OTHER	
OTHER	

Christmas Lunch or Dinner Menu

APPETIZER	
MAIN DISH	
SIDE ITEMS	
DESSERTS	
BEVERAGES	
OTHER	

Grocery List

X	#	ITEM	X	#	ITEM

Grocery List

X	#	ITEM	X	#	ITEM

To Do List

DONE	TO DO

To Do List

DONE	TO DO

Gifts to Give List

DATE NEEDED	DATE GIVEN	RECIPIENT	GIFT GIVEN

Gifts Received List

DATE RECEIVED	THANK YOU NOTE SENT	GIVER	GIFT RECEIVED

CARD SENT:	NAME:	PHONE:
CARD RCVD:	ADDRESS:	

CARD SENT:	NAME:	PHONE:
CARD RCVD:	ADDRESS:	

CARD SENT:	NAME:	PHONE:
CARD RCVD:	ADDRESS:	

CARD SENT:	NAME:	PHONE:
CARD RCVD:	ADDRESS:	

CARD SENT:	NAME:	PHONE:
CARD RCVD:	ADDRESS:	

CARD SENT:	NAME:	PHONE:
CARD RCVD:	ADDRESS:	

CARD SENT:	NAME:	PHONE:
CARD RCVD:	ADDRESS:	

CARD SENT:	NAME:	PHONE:
CARD RCVD:	ADDRESS:	

CARD SENT:		NAME:	PHONE:
CARD RCVD:		ADDRESS:	

CARD SENT:		NAME:	PHONE:
CARD RCVD:		ADDRESS:	

CARD SENT:		NAME:	PHONE:
CARD RCVD:		ADDRESS:	

CARD SENT:		NAME:	PHONE:
CARD RCVD:		ADDRESS:	

CARD SENT:		NAME:	PHONE:
CARD RCVD:		ADDRESS:	

CARD SENT:		NAME:	PHONE:
CARD RCVD:		ADDRESS:	

CARD SENT:		NAME:	PHONE:
CARD RCVD:		ADDRESS:	

CARD SENT:		NAME:	PHONE:
CARD RCVD:		ADDRESS:	

CARD SENT:		NAME:	PHONE:
CARD RCVD:		ADDRESS:	

CARD SENT:		NAME:	PHONE:
CARD RCVD:		ADDRESS:	

CARD SENT:		NAME:	PHONE:
CARD RCVD:		ADDRESS:	

CARD SENT:		NAME:	PHONE:
CARD RCVD:		ADDRESS:	

CARD SENT:		NAME:	PHONE:
CARD RCVD:		ADDRESS:	

CARD SENT:		NAME:	PHONE:
CARD RCVD:		ADDRESS:	

CARD SENT:		NAME:	PHONE:
CARD RCVD:		ADDRESS:	

CARD SENT:		NAME:	PHONE:
CARD RCVD:		ADDRESS:	

CARD SENT:		NAME:	PHONE:
CARD RCVD:		ADDRESS:	

CARD SENT:		NAME:	PHONE:
CARD RCVD:		ADDRESS:	

CARD SENT:		NAME:	PHONE:
CARD RCVD:		ADDRESS:	

CARD SENT:		NAME:	PHONE:
CARD RCVD:		ADDRESS:	

CARD SENT:		NAME:	PHONE:
CARD RCVD:		ADDRESS:	

CARD SENT:		NAME:	PHONE:
CARD RCVD:		ADDRESS:	

CARD SENT:		NAME:	PHONE:
CARD RCVD:		ADDRESS:	

CARD SENT:		NAME:	PHONE:
CARD RCVD:		ADDRESS:	

CARD SENT:	NAME:	PHONE:
CARD RCVD:	ADDRESS:	

CARD SENT:	NAME:	PHONE:
CARD RCVD:	ADDRESS:	

CARD SENT:	NAME:	PHONE:
CARD RCVD:	ADDRESS:	

CARD SENT:	NAME:	PHONE:
CARD RCVD:	ADDRESS:	

CARD SENT:	NAME:	PHONE:
CARD RCVD:	ADDRESS:	

CARD SENT:	NAME:	PHONE:
CARD RCVD:	ADDRESS:	

CARD SENT:	NAME:	PHONE:
CARD RCVD:	ADDRESS:	

CARD SENT:	NAME:	PHONE:
CARD RCVD:	ADDRESS:	

CARD SENT:	NAME:	PHONE:
CARD RCVD:	ADDRESS:	

CARD SENT:	NAME:	PHONE:
CARD RCVD:	ADDRESS:	

CARD SENT:	NAME:	PHONE:
CARD RCVD:	ADDRESS:	

CARD SENT:	NAME:	PHONE:
CARD RCVD:	ADDRESS:	

CARD SENT:	NAME:	PHONE:
CARD RCVD:	ADDRESS:	

CARD SENT:	NAME:	PHONE:
CARD RCVD:	ADDRESS:	

CARD SENT:	NAME:	PHONE:
CARD RCVD:	ADDRESS:	

CARD SENT:	NAME:	PHONE:
CARD RCVD:	ADDRESS:	

Record some of your favorite Christmas memories or traditions below:

_____

_____

_____

_____

_____

_____

_____

_____

_____

_____

_____

_____

_____

_____

_____

_____

_____

_____

_____

_____

_____

_____

Record some of your favorite Christmas memories or traditions below:

_____

_____

_____

_____

_____

_____

_____

_____

_____

_____

_____

_____

_____

_____

_____

_____

_____

_____

_____

_____

_____

_____

_____

_____

_____

Record some of your favorite Christmas memories or traditions below:

_____

_____

_____

_____

_____

_____

_____

_____

_____

_____

_____

_____

_____

_____

_____

_____

_____

_____

_____

_____

_____

_____

_____

Record some of your favorite Christmas memories or traditions below:

_____
_____
_____
_____
_____
_____
_____
_____
_____
_____
_____
_____
_____
_____
_____
_____
_____
_____
_____
_____
_____
_____
_____

Wrapping Supplies

✓	#	ITEM	✓	#	ITEM
		Rolls of Wrapping Paper			
		Gifts Sacks, Small			
		Gift Sacks, Medium			
		Gift Sacks, Large			
		Tape			
		Tissue Paper			
		Wrapping Boxes			
		Gift Tags			
		Bows			
		Curling Ribbon			
		Flat Ribbon			
		Small Ornaments			
		Package Decorations			
		Food Safe Bags			
		Food Tins			
		Boxes for Baked Goods			
		Packing Boxes (for mailing)			
		Packing Tape (for mailing)			
		Permanent Markers/Pen for Tags			

IDEA GENERATORS

Weekly Task List

WEEK 1

WEEK 2

WEEK 3

WEEK 4

WEEK 5

SUNDAY	MONDAY	TUESDAY	WEDNESDAY	THURSDAY	FRIDAY	SATURDAY

SUNDAY	MONDAY	TUESDAY	WEDNESDAY	THURSDAY	FRIDAY	SATURDAY

_____   _____

_____   _____

_____   _____

_____   _____

_____   _____

_____   _____

SUNDAY	MONDAY	TUESDAY	WEDNESDAY	THURSDAY	FRIDAY	SATURDAY

SUNDAY	MONDAY	TUESDAY	WEDNESDAY	THURSDAY	FRIDAY	SATURDAY

Place Cards

Gift Tags

To:

From:

To:

From:

To:

From:

To:

From:

To:

From:

To:

From:

To:

From:

To:

From:

COUPON

This certificate entitles you to:

To:

From:

COUPON

This certificate entitles you to:

To:

From:

Handmade Tags

Handmade just for you!

To:

From:

Handmade just for you!

To:

From:

Handmade just for you!

To:

From:

Handmade just for you!

To:

From:

Handmade just for you!

To:

From:

Notes

Notes

Notes

Made in the USA
Coppell, TX
29 October 2020